The Girl Who Wanted To Know God

The Girl Who Wanted To Know God

The Story of One Girl Who Went From Knowing About God to Knowing God

By Wade Galt

Possibility Infinity Publishing

ISBN 978-1-934108-19-2

To God...

Thank you for always being there for me.

These Ideas Work For Me...

I wouldn't call them beliefs because I'm not attached to them. I'm not ready to kill or die to prove I'm right or that someone else is wrong. This is not dogma, so there's no need for anyone to argue. I'm not suggesting I'm right or others are wrong. I may be incorrect. I'm not saying I hold the only truth, the ultimate truth, or even truth.

This book is a collection of ideas that feel true to me, that inspire me, and that work for me (based on what I can see in my life). I'd love to hear how these and other ideas work for you. I see this as a two-way learning relationship that we can both learn from. I'm not the teacher. You're not the student. We're just two people exploring ideas about the divine in hope of improving our lives and the world.

Please Accept My Humility and My Grandiosity

It is my only intention that this work brings you closer to peace, love, joy, happiness, and a greater connection with the divine. Please excuse my limitations as a writer as I attempt to do this. It is not my intention to make anyone feel wrong, uncomfortable, that they need to change, or feel anything other than fully loved, accepted and supported.

Please accept my grandiosity in wanting to address such a huge and important subject (and any apparent presumption that I'm right). Please also accept my humility in doing my best to make myself vulnerable by sharing something I think will make the world a better place. I honor all those people, organizations, religions, beliefs, rituals, and everything else that seeks to do the same,

At the same time, I remain excited, open-hearted and open-minded to seeing how we may grow, evolve, and change how we relate with the divine and each other to bring about even more peace, love, and happiness.

The Girl Who Wanted To Know God

The Girl Who Wanted To Know God

A girl woke up one day wanting to know God.

As the girl walked down the street

she saw an old woman.

"Good day," the old woman said. *"You seem to be looking for something. May I help you?"*

"I want to know God," she told the old woman.

"Sit here for a while," the old woman said, *"and you shall get to know God."*

The girl sat for a few moments when a young lady walked up to her.

"What are you doing?"

the young lady asked.

"I want to know God," she told the young lady.

"I can teach you how to be a good person," the young lady replied. "Come with me, and you will learn the ways of the righteous."

The girl thanked the old woman and said, "I'm going to learn to be a righteous woman."

The old woman replied, "You will learn much from this young lady."

The girl returned two years later to the same place where she met the old woman.

"Did you find what you were looking for?" asked the old woman.

"*I have practiced many disciplines,*" *replied the girl.* "*I have recited the verses in the correct way. I have sinned less and less every day. I have apologized to God for the sins I committed.*"

"So did you get to know God?"

asked the old woman.

"I learned a great deal about being righteous," answered the girl, "but I didn't really get to know God. I want to know God."

"Sit here for a while,"

the old woman said,

"and you shall get to know God."

The girl sat for a few moments when two young men walked up to her.

"What are you doing?"

asked one of the young men.

"*I want to know God,*" *she told*

the young man.

"Come with us, and you can learn everything about God," the young man promised.

"You know God?" the girl asked.

"We have studied for years," the other replied, "and we know everything humans have ever written about God."

Again the girl thanked the old woman and said, "I'm going to learn about God."

The old woman replied, "You will learn much from these men."

The girl returned two years later to the same place where she met the old woman.

"Did you find what you were looking for?" asked the old woman.

The girl replied, "I have learned many things about God. I have learned what we believe he wants for us. I have learned how we believe he created us. I have learned how we like to worship him. I have learned what many believe are the correct ways to pray to him, and I have memorized all the words humans have written about him."

"So did you get to know God?"

asked the old woman.

"*I learned a great deal about what humans think of God,*" *answered the girl,* "*but I didn't really get to know God. I want to know God.*"

"Sit here for a while,"
the old woman said,
"and you shall get to know God."

The girl sat for a few moments when a young boy walked up to her.

"What are you doing?" he asked.

"I want to know God," she told the young boy.

"My friends and I are going to build houses for the homeless," he replied. "Come with us, and you will learn to give selflessly and completely of yourself."

Again the girl thanked the old woman and said, "I'm going to learn to give completely of myself and be selfless."

The old woman replied, "You will learn much from this boy."

The girl returned two years later to the same place where she met the old woman.

"Did you find what you were looking for?" asked the old woman.

"I built houses for those who had no place to live," replied the girl. "I helped people learn to take care of their needs for shelter and warmth. I helped provide shelter for thousands of people."

"*So did you get to know God?*"

asked the old woman.

"I learned a great deal about building houses and giving to others," answered the girl, "but I didn't really get to know God. I want to know God."

"Sit here for a while,"

the old woman said,

"and you shall get to know God."

The girl sat for a few moments when a group of men walked up to her.

"What are you doing?"

one of the men asked.

"I want to know God," the girl told the man.

"We are going to heal the sick," he replied. "Come with us, and you will learn to take care of the needy."

Once again the girl thanked the old woman and said, "I'm going to learn to heal the sick."

The old woman replied, "You will learn much from these men."

The girl returned two years later to the same place where she met the old woman.

"Did you find what you were looking for?" asked the old woman.

"I helped cure people who were sick with disease," replied the girl. "I helped people learn to eat properly to nourish themselves and prevent illness. I taught them to be healthy and live long. The number of deaths in the village I worked in has gone down by hundreds every year I have been there."

"So did you get to know God?"

asked the old woman.

"*I learned a great deal about healing disease,*" *answered the girl,* "*but I didn't really get to know God. I want to know God.*"

"Sit here for a while,"

the old woman said,

"and you shall get to know God."

The girl sat for a few moments
when a group of women walked up
to her.

"What are you doing?"

one of the women asked.

"I want to know God," she told

the woman.

"We are going to feed the hungry," she replied. "Come with us, and you will learn to take care of the poor."

The girl paused for a moment and thanked the woman by saying, "Thank you for the offer. I wish you well in your journey, but I do not wish to take care of the poor. My goal is to know God."

The women looked at her curiously.
The old woman said nothing and
smiled.

The girl grew still for a while and did nothing.

After a while, she noticed a butterfly and wondered how such a delicate creature could fly.

She felt a sense of awe over such a

miraculous creation.

Then she noticed the clouds in the sky and was amazed by the thought that these floating islands held water in them, yet they did not fall.

She felt a sense of wonder over such an ingenious design.

Next she saw a group of ants working together, and she marveled at their cooperation and single-mindedness of purpose.

She felt a sense of astonishment over such beautiful harmony.

Finally, she saw a light in the eyes of the old woman, and she could not believe the amount of love she saw in the old woman's eyes.

She immediately felt a sense of unity with everyone and everything.

"*Did you find what you were looking for?*" asked the old woman.

"Yes, I did," replied the young girl. "I have now found what I first sought so many years ago."

"It seemed to take a bit longer than you intended," observed the old woman as she smiled.

"*Perhaps,*" *said the girl.* "*But it took just as long as I really wanted it to take.*"

"Indeed," said the old woman. "I know that is true. How do you know that is true?"

The girl began, "When I started out I was more interested in feeling righteous than I was in knowing God. I got what I wanted, and many people observed how righteous I was."

"I see," said the old woman.

"Then I was more interested in learning information about God and understanding what humans believe about God," continued the girl. "I learned and memorized many of humankind's ideas about God, and I proved my intelligence."

"This is true," replied the old woman.

"Then I wanted to prove I was a kind person," said the girl. "I gave my life to serving those without homes and I called them 'needy' even though I needed them to feel good about myself just as much as they needed me to help them get shelter."

"Quite insightful," remarked the

old woman.

"Then I had a need to prove I was powerful," continued the girl. "I learned how to postpone death and felt god-like in the process, though I never felt I knew God."

"I couldn't have said it better myself," agreed the old woman. "So now what do you want?"

"I want to be with God," the girl replied. "I think I will stay here."

As the girl said this, she looked around and noticed that all the other people around her had the same loving look she saw in the old woman's eyes. They always had it. It was just not easy for her to see before.

"You will be with me even if I leave this place, won't you?" the girl asked the old woman.

"I always have been with you," said the old woman, "And I always will." As she said this, the young girl saw all the travelers she had met along her journey, and they all had the same loving look in their eyes.

"*I guess I only saw you and got to know you when I truly wanted to,*" the girl concluded.

"Yes," the old woman replied. "And you will always see me and know me whenever you wish."

"Thank you," the girl said. "I now know what to do with my life."

"And what is that?" asked the old woman.

"Live with you in my heart always," she replied.

"What about all the books, teachings, and good deeds you have learned and lived?" asked the old woman.

"They are important, but they are not truly necessary," the girl replied. "As long as I keep you first in my heart always I will know how to live."

"And what about the homeless people, hungry people and sick people?" asked the old woman. "Don't they need you?"

"They don't really need me, though it felt great to think they did," the girl answered. "All they really need is to know God. I know they are in good hands."

"Do they even need to know God?"

asked the old woman.

"I don't think so," the girl replied.
"I imagine you will be there for
them regardless what they know."

"You know me well," the old woman replied. "So now what do you intend to do with your life?"

"At some point, I think I will focus on helping those who look like they could use help, but for now I think I will just focus on knowing you," the girl answered with a smile. "I'm pretty sure the rest of the details will come to me when I need to know them."

"Indeed they will," replied the old woman.

I'm Now Ready

I'm now ready to learn.

Oh, there's my teacher!

My teacher has been standing in front of me for years,
But I have been unwilling and unable to see him.

He didn't appear from anywhere.
He had always been right there.

I just decided to see him.

Suddenly, his teachings are so brilliant.
Suddenly, it all works.
Suddenly, I'm evolving.

Suddenly was not so sudden...
until it was.

The day was so dark...
until I opened my eyes.

The Girl Who Wanted To Know God

Acknowledgments

Thank you God... for being all I need. I know I forget sometimes, and I know I do not always live my life from this place of understanding. Thank you for being patient with me and for loving me at every step in the journey.

My intention is that all who read this book, including myself, will experience the joy, bliss and fulfillment that come from loving you, being loved by you, and truly knowing that you are all we need.

About the Author

Wade has led retreats and personal growth workshops, authored books on spirituality, personal growth, finance, parenting, business growth & more.

He has worked successfully as a life coach, 4-day work week mentor, organizational consultant, computer trainer, sales consultant, executive coach, speaker, mental health counselor, management consultant, software designer and programmer, author, business analyst, financial counselor, and in many other capacities.

Wade has a Bachelor's degree in Marketing and a Master's degree in Mental Health Counseling Psychology.

He lives happily with his wife and children.

His email address is wade@wadegalt.com .

Author Blog & Website

You may visit Wade's blog & website at www.wadegalt.com .

Also by Wade Galt

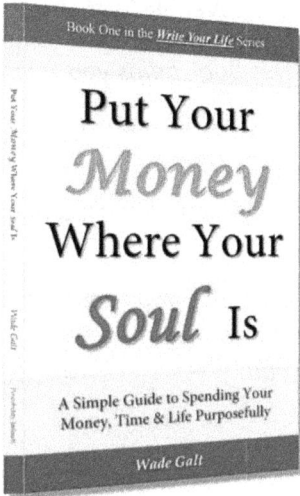

Put Your Money Where Your Soul Is

A Simple Guide to Spending Your Money, Time and Life Purposefully

Learn how to free up additional time, money and energy by redefining your relationships with money, time, people, and things.

Simple strategies, exercises & tools help you make powerful changes with very little effort or struggle.

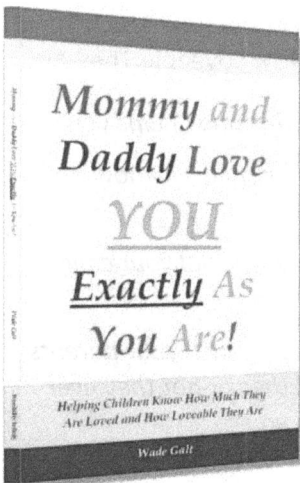

Mommy and Daddy Love You Exactly As You Are!

Helping Children Know How Much They Are Loved and How Loveable They Are

My hope is that this book helps you...

1) Let your child or children know how special they are.

2) Remember how special your child or children are.

3) Understand how much your parents love(d) you, whether or not they ever shared this with you.

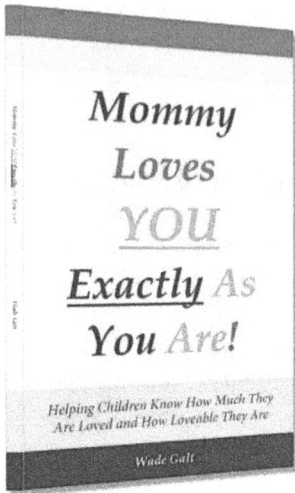

Mommy Loves You Exactly As You Are!

Helping Children Know How Much They Are Loved and How Loveable They Are

My hope is that this book helps you...

1) Let your child or children know how special they are.

2) Remember how special your child or children are.

3) Understand how much your parents love(d) you, whether or not they ever shared this with you.

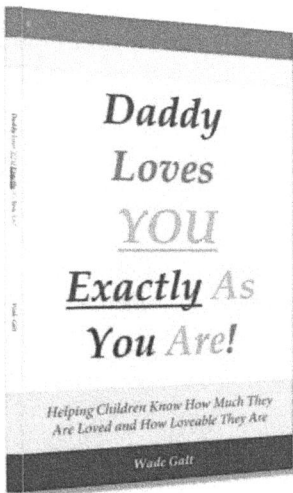

Daddy Loves You Exactly As You Are!

Helping Children Know How Much They Are Loved and How Loveable They Are

My hope is that this book helps you...

1) Let your child or children know how special they are.

2) Remember how special your child or children are.

3) Understand how much your parents love(d) you, whether or not they ever shared this with you.

The *God Equals Love* Book Series

(Free eBook Versions Available for All Books)

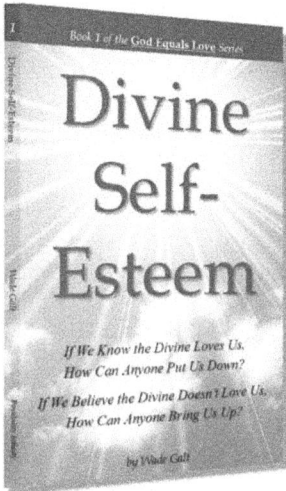

Book 1 - Divine Self-Esteem

Learning to Love Ourselves
the Way the Divine Loves Us

If we know the Divine loves us, how can anyone put us down?

If we believe the Divine doesn't love us, how can anyone bring us up?

Learn to see yourself through divinely loving eyes and catch a glimpse of the divinely-made miracle you are.

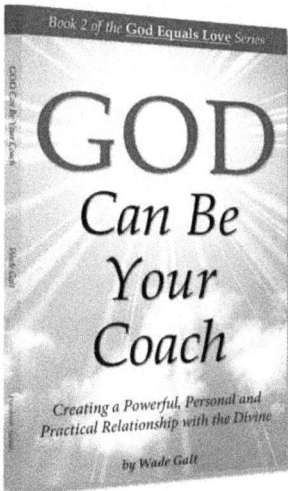

Book 2 - GOD Can Be Your Coach

Creating a Powerful, Personal and
Practical Relationship with the Divine

Create More Joy, Happiness, Love, Peace and Purpose in Your Life.

Learn One Simple Way to form a more powerful connection & relationship.

If You Knew You Could Connect with the Divine Anytime You Choose to Receive Guidance, Support, and Peace, Would You?

Will You?

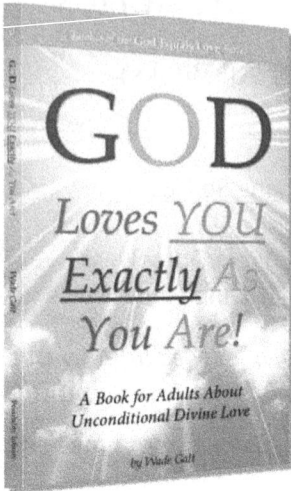

3 - GOD Loves You Exactly As You Are!

Understanding & Experiencing
Unconditional Divine Love

An Invitation to Consider & Experience the Life-Altering Understanding That You are Completely and Unconditionally Loved and Loveable EXACTLY AS YOU ARE!

What If God Loves You EXACTLY as You are?

How Would Understanding that Transform Your Life?

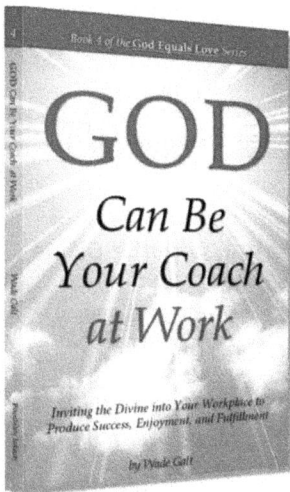

Book 4 - GOD Can Be Your Coach at Work

Inviting the Divine into Your Workplace to Produce Success, Enjoyment & Fulfillment

Few of us fully live our highest spiritual values in our workplace.

This is a source of frustration, shame, guilt & dissatisfaction for billions of us.

What if the divine actually wants us to experience life, love, joy, fulfillment, and abundance inside and outside our work?

What if the divine cares about our work simply because the divine cares for us?

This book is an invitation to work WITH the divine to create divinely inspired results for you and the world.

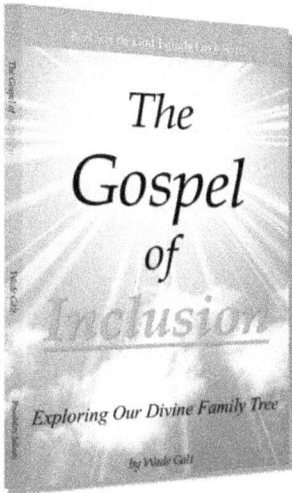

Book 5 - The Gospel of Inclusion

Exploring Our Divine Family Tree

Who is included in God's plan? Is it only people like me? Only people like you? What atrocities & apathy do we justify daily by declaring others are outside of God's chosen circle of people?

What if we really are part of one divine family? What would that mean? How would we have to change?

WARNING! Reading this book may lead you to (1) consider the possibility that we're all God's children and (2) do something about that. Proceed at your own risk!

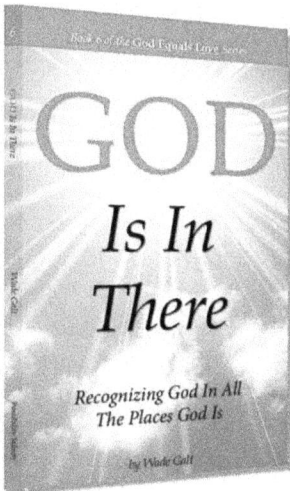

Book 6 - God Is In There

Recognizing God In All The Places God Is

If you could teach only one spiritual lesson, what would you teach?

What truth could you share that is so powerful, it would fundamentally transform the way others live?

There are a few core ideas that most spiritual traditions hold as true. Some believe that the most powerful and life-transforming truths are so self-evident and so obvious that all traditions agree about them.

This book contains one of those ideas.

7 - The Boy Who Wanted to Know God

The Story of One Boy Who Went from
  Knowing About God to Knowing God

*What would you be willing to do in
order to meet God?*

*Join a curious and excited young boy on
his journey to meeting the divine.*

You might meet God, too.

*The journey may be shorter and simpler
than you think.*

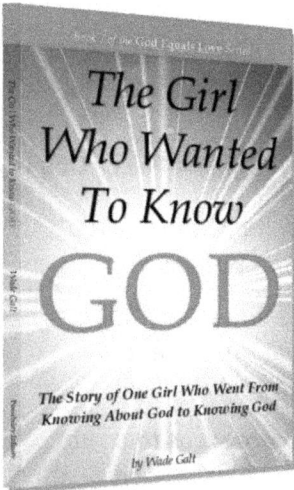

7 - The Girl Who Wanted to Know God

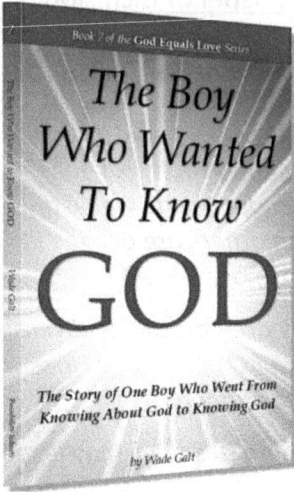

The Story of One Girl Who Went from
  Knowing About God to Knowing God

*What would you be willing to do in
order to meet God?*

*Join a curious and excited young girl on
her journey to meeting the divine.*

You might meet God, too.

*The journey may be shorter and simpler
than you think.*

Translated into Spanish (More to Come)

Autoestima Divina

Aprendiendo a Amarnos De la Forma en que Dios nos Ama

Si sabemos que el Divino nos ama, ¿cómo podemos sentirnos mal con nosotros mismos?

Si creemos que el Divino no nos ama, ¿cómo podemos sentirnos bien con nosotros mismos?

Aprender a verse a sí mismo a través de los ojos de amor de Dios y echar un vistazo a el milagro hecho de Dios-que eres.

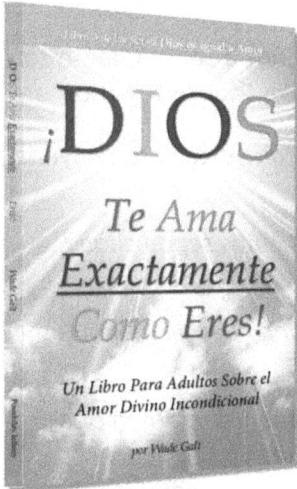

DIOS Te Ama Exactamente Como Eres

Un Libro Para Adultos Sobre el Amor Divino Incondicional

¿Y Si Dios te ama EXACTAMENTE como eres? ¿De que manera ese entendimiento transformaría tu vida?

Esto Es Una Simple Invitación... Para Considerar y Experimentar... Un Entendimiento de la Vida Alternativo...

Tú Eres Completa e Incondicionalmente... Amado y Adorable... EXACTAMENTE COMO ERES!

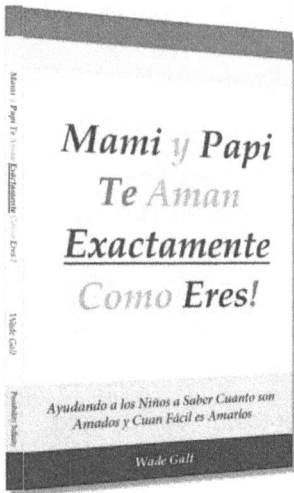

Mami y Papi Te Aman Exactamente Como Eres!

Ayudando a los Niños a Saber Cuanto son Amados y Cuan Fácil es Amarlos

Mi esperanza es que este libro te ayude a...

1) Hacer que tus niños sepan cuan especiales son.

2) Recordarte cuan especiales son tus niños.

3) Comprender cuanto te aman o te amaron tus padres ya sea que compartieran o no esto contigo.

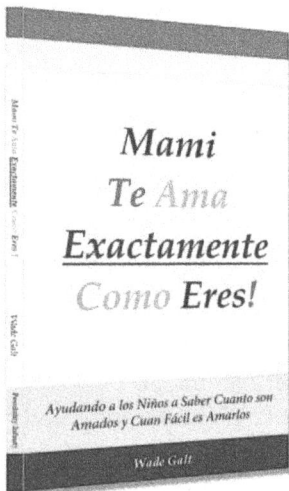

Mami Te Ama Exactamente Como Eres!

Ayudando a los Niños a Saber Cuanto son Amados y Cuan Fácil es Amarlos

Mi esperanza es que este libro te ayude a...

1) Hacer que tus niños sepan cuan especiales son.

2) Recordarte cuan especiales son tus niños.

3) Comprender cuanto te aman o te amaron tus padres ya sea que compartieran o no esto contigo.

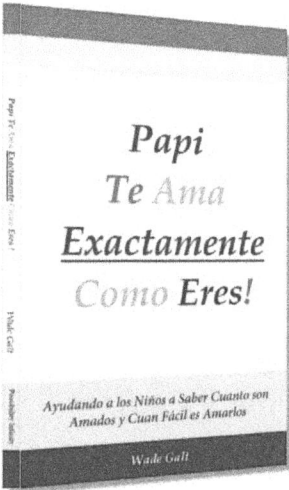

Papi Te Ama Exactamente Como Eres!

Ayudando a los Niños a Saber Cuanto son Amados y Cuan Fácil es Amarlos

Mi esperanza es que este libro te ayude a...

1) Hacer que tus niños sepan cuan especiales son.

2) Recordarte cuan especiales son tus niños.

3) Comprender cuanto te aman o te amaron tus padres ya sea que compartieran o no esto contigo.

To see these books and other books not listed here, visit www.wadegalt.com/books .

All profits from the sale of the GOD EQUALS LOVE books go to organizations and charities that seek to end unnecessary hunger and poverty.

New Book & Program Notifications

If you'd like to be emailed when we release new books, audios and other programs please visit www.wadegalt.com/notifiy to sign up for these notifications.

Share the Message & the Love

I hope this helps you see & feel how truly amazing and miraculous of a creation you are and how much the divine values you.

If you found the book to be helpful, would you please be so kind as to write a review on Amazon for the book or share the book on Facebook, Instagram, Twitter or other social media so others may know how it helped you?

Even if it's a super-short review, every little bit helps.

Thank you so much.

If there's anything I can do to help you further with this work, please email me at is wade@wadegalt.com .

All my best,

Wade

www.ingramcontent.com/pod-product-compliance
Lightning Source LLC
Chambersburg PA
CBHW070638030426
42337CB00020B/4061